Cartoons by Guindon

Hello, I'm Dick Guindon, the president of Guindco, just one in a team of hundreds who bring you those lovable cartoon characters that have made me, and (if you'll keep reading) can make you, *rich!*

I want you to become a cartoonist. That's right, you can become a cartoonist; rich, successful and beloved. It doesn't take great art talent, if that's what you're thinking; so don't hand me that. All it takes is *attitude!* For instance, Gary Trudeau, who draws Doonesbury, is a millionaire and can't draw hands. But he has a great *attitude!* Charles Shultz, creator of Peanuts, owns much of Northern California and he

doesn't know how to shade. But he, too, has a great *attitude*. Who among you hasn't said to himself, "Gosh! I bet even I could draw Ziggy!" Of course you can.

Why not begin right now? Sit down and draw some cartoons and then, and this is the important part, turn out a chain book! That's what I've done, and here's how it works. Send this book to 20 of your friends. They, in turn, send 20 copies to their friends. It helps if you tell them they might die if they break the chain. At the end of the year, you could receive hundreds of copies of this book in the mail! It's working for me. Why not make it work for you?

Richard Guindon

The Beginning:
For some of us, it's important to be in on the beginning of anything new that comes along.

"Really? I'm shallow too!"

"Oh, pretty quiet tonight. About 7:30 my leg went to sleep,
that's about it."

Some superficial people applauding a new trend.

"Give me your mantra."

"Nice workmanship, but clearly a forgery."

Wine tip: Pouring wine down your tie to a glass helps aerate it.

"Good Night, Betamax. Good Night, dirt bike. Good Night, Cuisinart. Good Night. . ."

A man with a 10-speed bike fed up with making all those decisions.

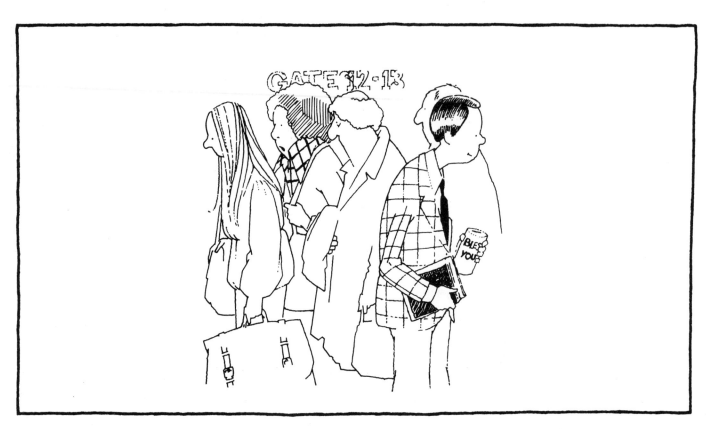

"What is it exactly those people believe in—air travel?"

"Do you want something to color while I'm getting ready?"

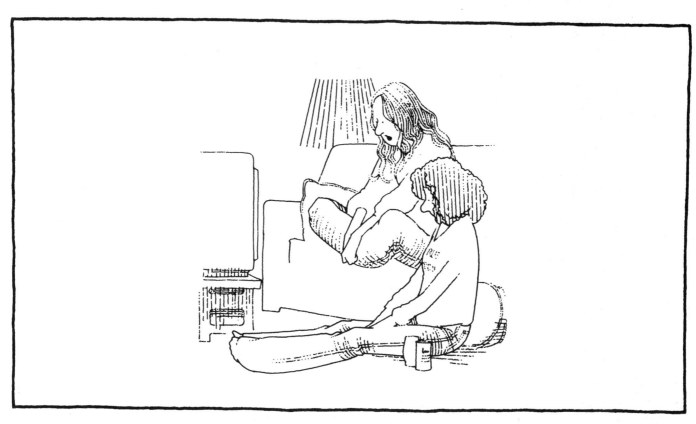

"This is another one of those shows that would be enhanced if they added a chimpanzee."

"The camera shot from inside the room is of Ingrid, looking out the window at Thule, who is in the yard. The room is very sparsely furnished and a clock is ticking in the background. And get this, the only motion is the curtains billowing slightly in the breeze. For 5 minutes that's all we see but it seems like forever because what I think Bergman is trying to tell us here. . ."

A nice guy finishing last.

"Once again: What have you done with Anne Klein and why are you wearing her clothes?"

Beauty Tip: Don't do this.

*"I liked it because you can read it with both the TV and
the radio on."*

*"I don't remember the entire evening but we began at, let's see...
Harry's Bar. Then we hit...Galileo's..."*

"If I can't be honest with you, Carl, this relationship doesn't stand much of a chance."

"Did you know you can't strip plastic?"

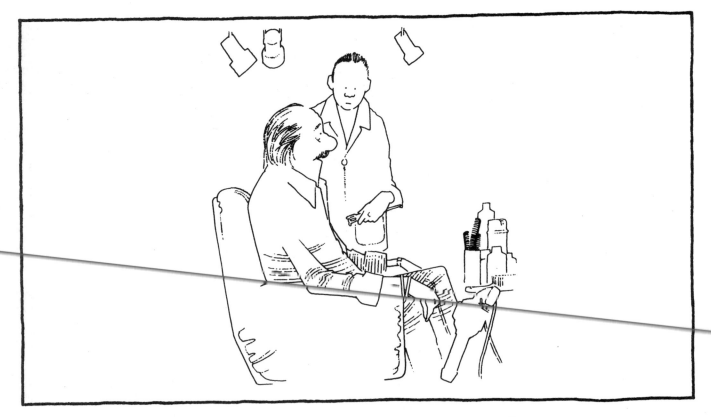

"Do you think I'm too old to wear my hair short?"

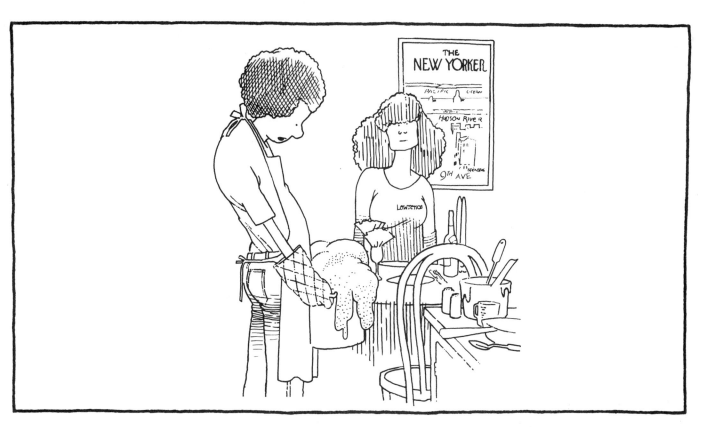

"The recipe I got for two was in metric units so I had to wing it a little."

"I didn't know North Dakota made a wine."

"Boy! It takes all kinds, don't it."

"I used to be a very poor poet until I had a fire and collected the insurance. That gave me a start in the dulcimer business and I must say it's treated me rather well."

*"It just occurred to me that if I were a German shepherd,
I'd be near death."*

"Tonight, I want the entire evening to be on my karma."

"What goes in this? It doesn't say."

*"Hey, how do you guys like your pick-up? Boy, we'd be just
lost without ours!"*

"Before you begin cooking your brown rice, it helps if you pause for a moment to consider the nature of existence."

"If you read the decals on all six glasses you know the complete history of Western thought."

"Merv Griffin looks like the kind of guy who would ask Merv Griffin for an autograph."

"Gee, I sure like your parents."

"I sometimes get into moods that feel very much like your dog looks."

*"The remark you've just made has hurt me and I'm feeling
anger toward you."*

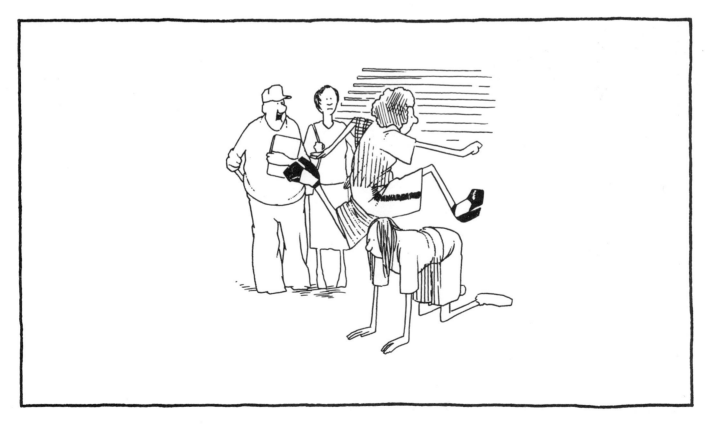

*"Of course, the women's athletic program isn't everything we'd
like it to be."*

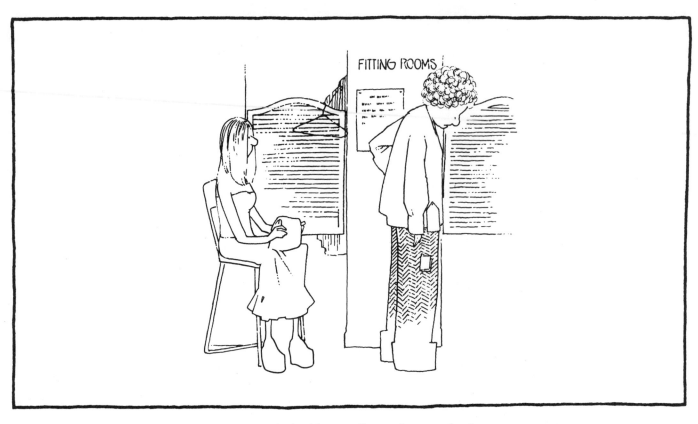

"I hate being so. . .indecisive. Well, not hate. . .that's too strong a word. Sometimes I don't mind being indecisive. . .I don't LOVE it, you know. . ."

"I was up late reading the instructions on how to operate this shirt."

"It's OK by me, but I hope you've thought this over. Marriage is a semi-serious step."

"Wait! Don't tell me. . .I know the face. . . ."

"Did you know that Campbell's suggests we heat this stuff up first?"

"If I were to live each day thinking it was my last, I think I'd be depressed all the time."

"Well, Pumpkin, in order to understand Charlie the Tuna, we first have to explain about something called a 'death wish.'"

"Harvey, one of the pieces of your suit is missing."

"Stardom was pretty tough to handle at 15, but at 16, I started to put it all together so that now at 17 I feel I've grown enough to take the pressure. But one thing will never change. And that is—no way, no how, is anybody ever going to make me eat liver."

"This is tough. I'm on a diet in which I can't eat any foods that have vowels."

"Why are you dressed like a drug dealer?"

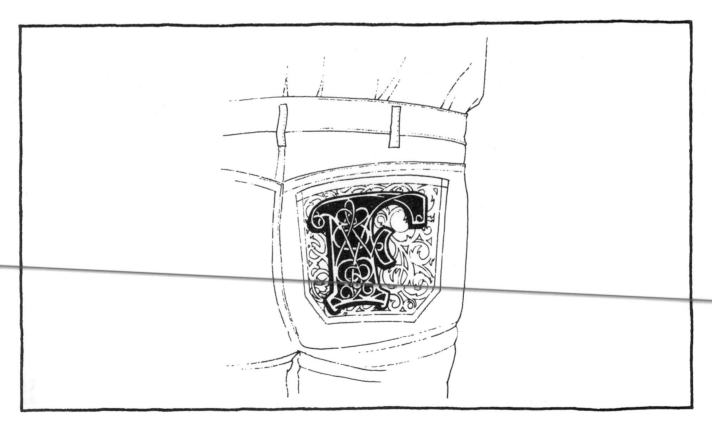

Designer jeans made by the monks at the Abbey of Saint Francis.

"I don't want to eat in a warehouse. I work in a warehouse!"

"I think I just took the cotton with the aspirin."

Fashion tip: Vertical stripes make you look taller, thinner, but not a whole lot.

"You still have your spoon but your little knife and fork have fallen off your necklace."

"Leave it—I'll write you another one."

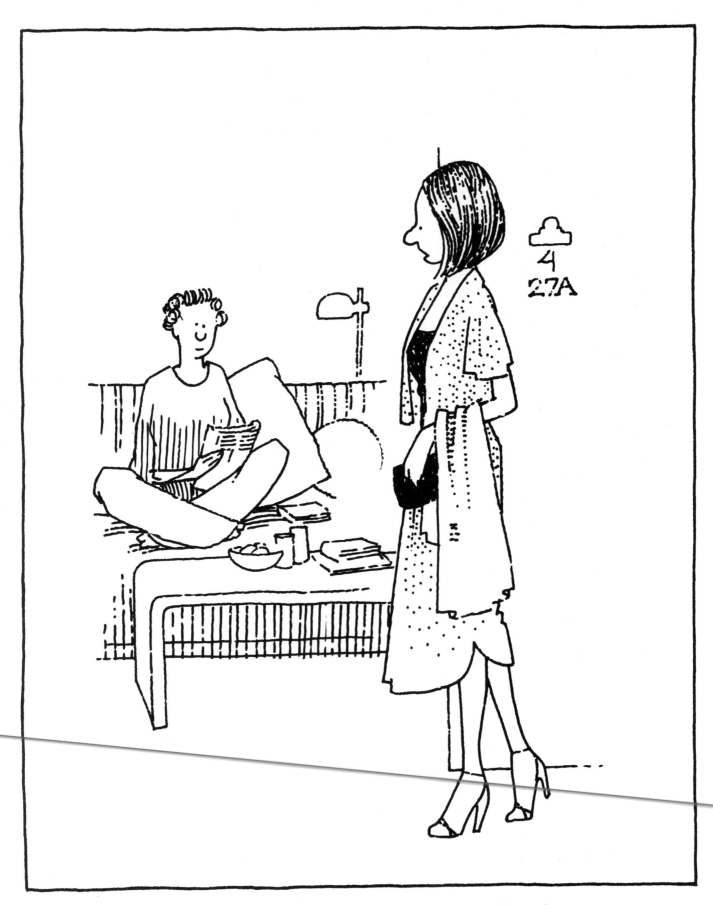

*"He turned out to be 28 years old and he had braces on his teeth.
You'd have thought his parents would have remembered."*

"I'll have the cauliflower soup, a zucchini sandwich on five grain bread, cider, and a side order of preservatives."

"Be careful of those paper plates. I've just washed them."

"How do you spell 'sincerely'?"

The Middle:
Some people are more comfortable living life in the middle, surrounded by those things that are familiar to them.

Casserole Eunice Benson

2 cups cooked macaroni
1 can tuna
1 can cream of mushroom soup

Combine ingredients and heat in oven at 350° for
12 minutes. (Serves 4.)

"Someone tried to cut us off in traffic and Flo mooned him."

Ned Gelderman horsing around with Mrs. Gelderman.

"Theo hated disco long before it caught on with the young people
in this country."

"I am wisdom. I am truth. I am woman."

"I'm afraid I just melted one of your shirts."

"Before we begin this hearing into just who keeps leaving the toilet seat up, the chair wants to caution the witnesses about any outburst during the testimony."

"Now this little sweetheart can save you a bundle on repairs."

"Actually, it's a very clever and slightly more expensive American imitation of the Japanese model."

"And then you know what she says to me? She says, 'What do you want for dinner?' It's eight A.M. and I don't even have my feet on the floor yet. . . ."

"Ethel, conversation is only a cheap trick for drawing attention to one's self."

*"Accepting the award for Laurence Olivier is our own
Betty Jo Burenski."*

*"We don't talk about Star Wars at the dinner table, Dear, because
Mommy and Daddy hate Star Wars."*

"Well. . .David. . .Sharon tells us that you're in the mime business."

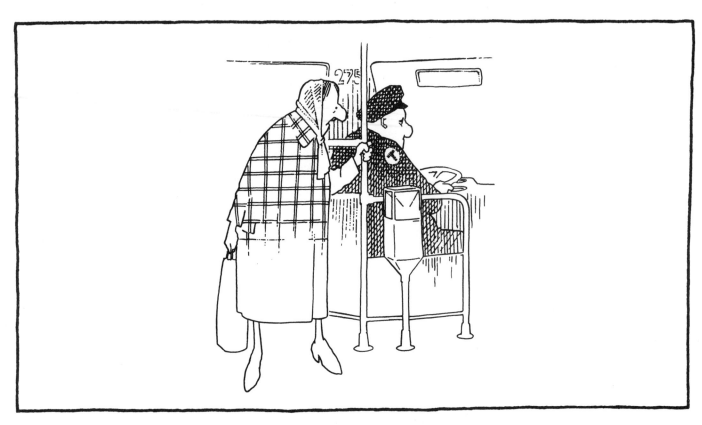

"You drive this bus like you're stealing it."

*"Have you ever noticed that everybody, no matter how faintly,
resembles someone famous? Except Bertram here, of course."*

"That's one of my good coasters you've just gotten all wet."

"Have you any idea how much your dollar has depreciated since you've entered this store?"

"I've called this press conference because I can no longer be silent about Orville's personal habits."

"A truly mature person can carry his fun inside him."

"I'll go along with that."

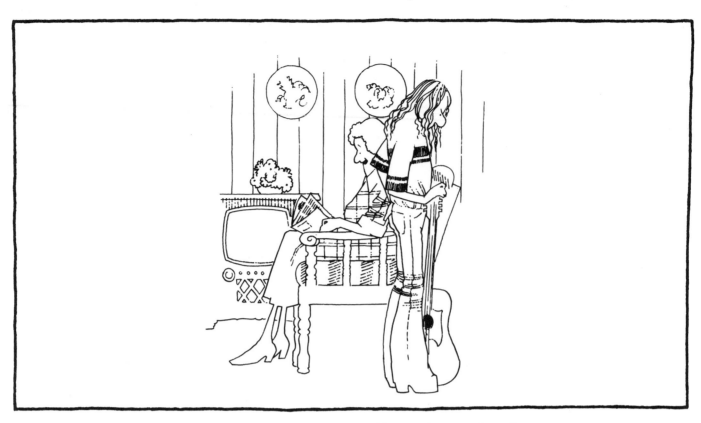

"That's nice. Who have you paid your dues to, dear?"

*"Do you think twelve dollars was too much to pay for
an original Picasso?"*

"Say, isn't that Bianca Jagger over there?"
"No."

"OK, I'm leaving now, and the first person who says 'Have a nice day' stops one."

"I'll go to the door. You start barking."

"Are you the same Esther Filmore who entered a contest with a recipe for Tuna Olé knowing full well that said contest was void where prohibited by law?"

"I hate the idea that underneath their clothes people go around nude."

"Who me? I'm just here plugging my book."

"Used to be, at fifteen dollars a plate—you'd be at a fund-raiser."

"Nowadays, it seems like everyone is a star."

*"Our guest tonight is a woman who is the author of three children.
She's a little bit nervous so let's give a great big welcome to Helen
Ann Ferguson. Ladies and Gentlemen—Let's hear it!"*

"Sure, everyone wants to save the whales, but not one voice is raised on behalf of the plankton!"

"I guess the fast-food business has pretty much reached the saturation point."

"You mean this is a real person and not my conscience?"

"Let's eat out at a nice 'Please wait. Hostess will seat you' place."

"Then perhaps you know my nephew in Detroit. He's gay too."

"It's not easy, being a nutritionist off duty. People watch you like a hawk."

"I won't be going back with you, Marvin."

*"Tonight's after-dinner speaker is a poet, shop teacher, and
C.B. radio operator. . . ."*

"They're collectables because I say they're collectables."

"I saw you coming up the walk on my radar range."

"Don't feed him or he'll follow you home."

*"You know, in all these years I haven't heard my Henry say a bad
word about anybody."*

"Martial arts. Isn't that your old high school?"

"How many people do you know who have actually READ their entire insurance policy and are prepared to discuss it intelligently?"

"OK! Where's *my* Womens Wear Daily?"

"In 1958, Murray found a genie in a bottle. For his three wishes he
got a fall-out shelter, an Edsel, and $10,000 a year."

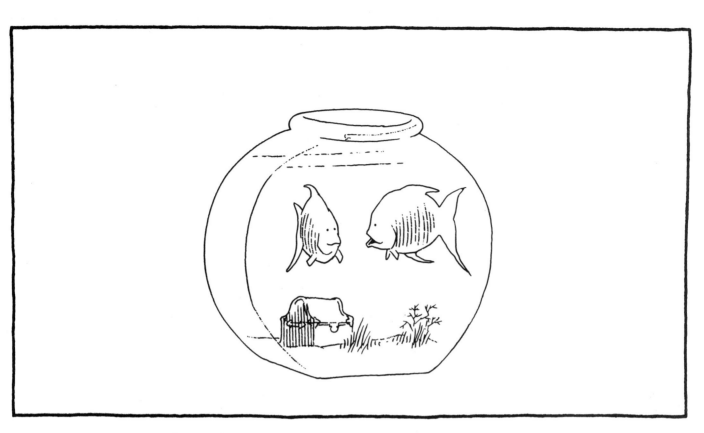

"If I'm right in my guess that this is the Atlantic, then we're the biggest fish in the world."

"Hello. I'm your appetite."

Skip Hogmier, the Carpet King, is so entertaining on T.V. that his commercials are now sponsored by the Ford Foundation.

"If you're bored, Dear, why not go down to the all-night grocery store and watch the hold-up?"

"The thing I like best about winter is that my feet don't sweat."

"Is that a new outfit or a cure for hiccups?"

"It was ten years ago today that I canceled my subscription to Vogue.*"*

"My Otto is not only against killing animals but he absolutely refuses to wear any item of clothing made of seafood."

"Something a lot of people don't understand about living in a small town is that you've got to make your own fun."

"Is Hollywood Modern still modern?"

"And to think that he got that way without the help of any chemicals."

"If you let me have my way all the time, I'll like myself better. Then I'll be easier to live with."

"Needle pointing is a hobby! Macramé is a hobby. Whistling is not a hobby!"

*"Honey, wouldn't you like something else for your birthday besides
a file cabinet?"*

*60 thousand spectators explode into a frenzy as Norton Fermin, a
retired T.V. repairman, single-handedly defeats the World Cup
horse shoe team.*

Orton Burton takes a day off from his upholstery business to rid the good dwarfs of Agar, the scourge of Friendly Forest.

*"We can't afford to send you to college, but we can give you bus
fare so you can join the Moonies."*

"Why don't we kick around what we paid for our houses and what they're worth now."

"It's been a while since we met anybody new unless you count those people we waved to on that float."

"Say, isn't that Melvin Levine behind those Foster Grants?"

"If you don't learn to read, you'll never be able to find out what's going to be on television."

"Have you seen a Frisbee?"

"How do people plead insanity? Who's gonna believe a crazy person?"

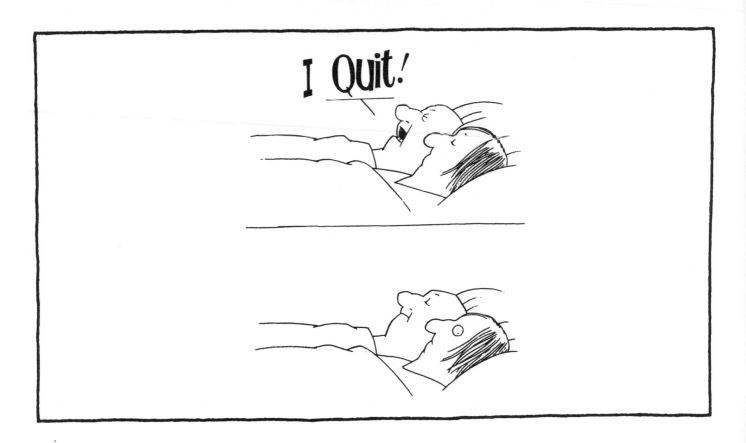

*"Who will be Miss 3207 N. Lincoln, Apartment 6?
The tension mounts. . . ."*

"It hovered for a few minutes and then landed and when the hatch opened some very odd little people came out who looked like they came from California."

*"Are you going to subscribe to the Time-Life series on the Etruscans
or can I throw this?"*

"Does it ever bother you that everything in our refrigerator is dead?"

"Now, do you have to send this money straight to Japan?"

"I'm leaving home. Will you help sponsor my walk?"

"OK! Everybody's gonna be careful not to hit John Denver or we'll probably never hear the end of it."

"And there, above the fireplace, I see a big fish on a plaque."

"Tell me, what considerations go into choosing just the right rock to paint a smile face on?"

*"I can't understand your risking your life for me, Mr. Bradley.
I'm only a fifth echelon Mert."*

"You cut a design in a potato, dip it in paint, and go bananas."

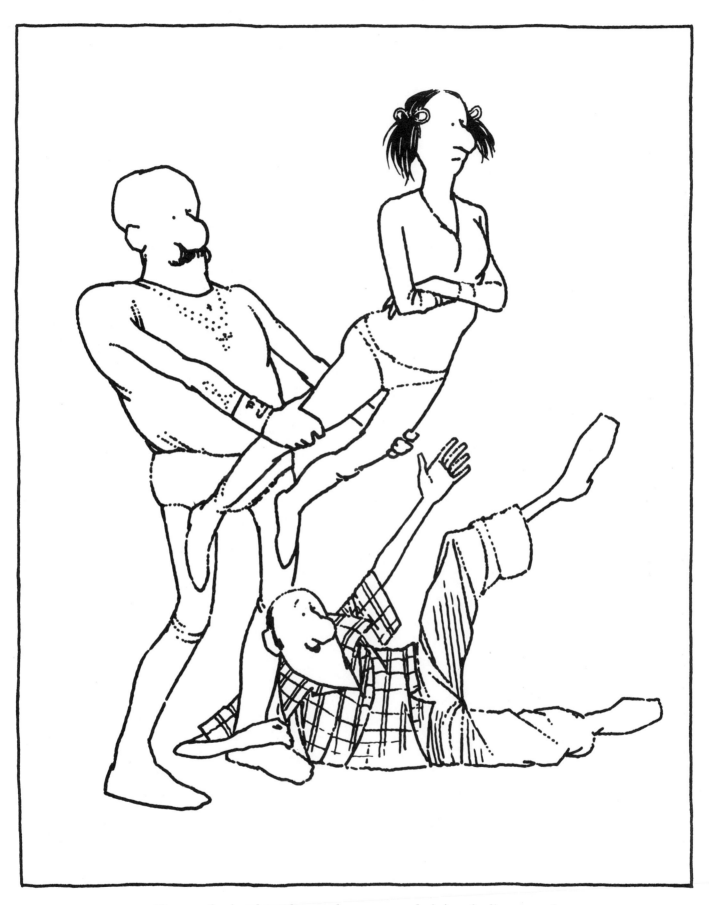

Two professional acrobats and some guy who's just fooling around.

The End:
Some people are on the fringe or end of the culture, not because they are trying to be different but because they are different.

"I'm laid back. You're laid back. Let's write a book about how we got there."

"You'll like Hiram's friend, Bill. He's a notary public, which means
he's probably very well read."

*Famous Imposters: Waldo Gordon, a high-school dropout, using
various aliases, has passed himself off as a dishwasher, a janitor, a
projectionist in a disco, and a car wash attendant, all without
ever being detected!*

*"Frankly, Bea, without some help, I'm not sure how much longer I
can hold this chapter of the Eddie Fisher Fan Club together."*

*"They have little Bobby and they want eight dollars—
what do you think?"*

"As our car was being stolen, he runs after it and takes
down the license."

"Actually, my mother used to think big feet were a sign that I'd
grow up to be tall."

"Betty? It's me, Darrell. Darrell 'Lady of Spain' Farley."

"How would you like to get on the endangered species list?"

Can Henry Netland of the U.S. Olympic team challenge the traditional dominance of the Italians in the Tossed Salad?

A little ostentatious. A big ostentatious.

After 1 week
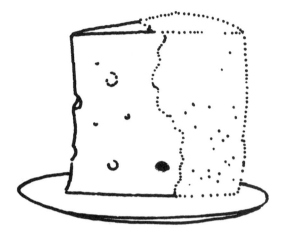

After 2 weeks

After 3 weeks

After 4 weeks

Consumer Tip: Chesse that begins showing a gray fuzz can be made more attractive by using Grecian Formula 44.

"Chapter Number One. Tell nobody that you have purchased and
are reading this book!"

"Pick, pick, pick. You're just like all the others."

"Honey, guess what? Your haircut's come back in."

"I guess you would have preferred being cloned by somebody with
a little more flash."

"It's dress-up, so wear your Nehru jacket."

Harvey Horse is writing a self-help book that will teach you how to
dominate any situation and bend others to your will with the
use of a gun.

"Why don't we offer to take in a little nuclear waste?"

*"Either you take this Susan B. Anthony dollar or I make
a citizen's arrest."*

"Because I've always been told that policemen are my friends—that's why I think we ought to have dinner and catch a show together."

In catching a carp, remember to bring it in to your body.

"Still nothing new from Paul Revere and the Raiders?"

"If we can put a man on the moon, why couldn't it have been you?"

*"If they do offer me the Johnny Carson show, it would mean giving
up Tuesday night bingo."*

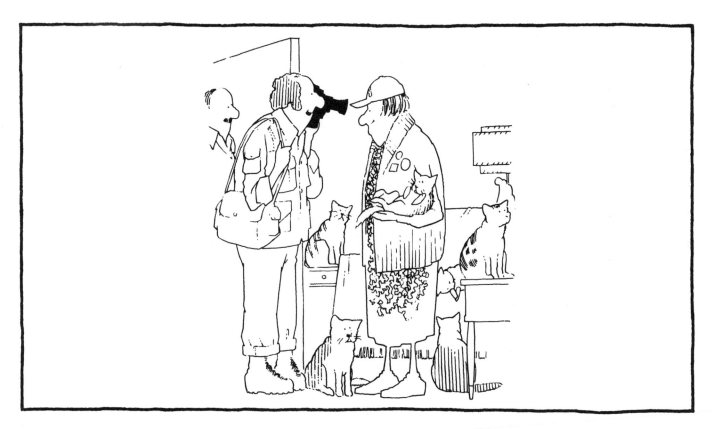

"Hi! We're from the National Geographic Society."

"I used to have an outfit just like that—only new."

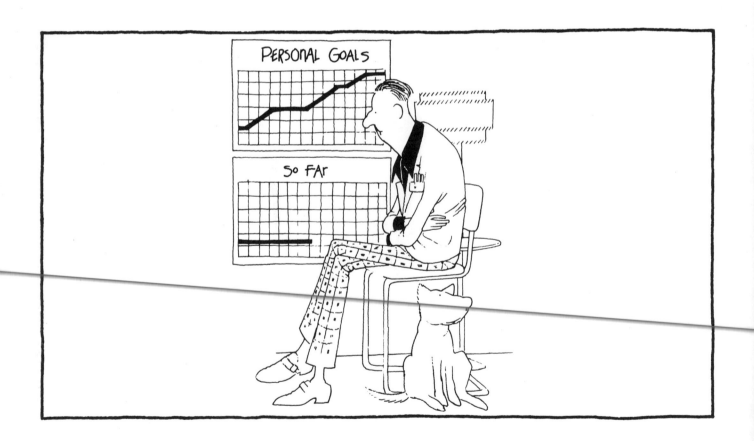

"We've got it—Punk Polka!"

"Look, Dad, a mosquito only has a life expectancy of four weeks,
so I, for one, intend to play it for laughs."

"Honey, do you think there will be much demand for a one man show featuring an imitation of Harold Stassen?"

"Don't go falling for me, Toots—I'm trouble."

"Oh, excuse me. I thought you were someone I knew."

"It must be pretty good stuff—you get a deposit back on the bottle."

Police artist sketch: The Laughing Shoplifter.

"I'm not asking for myself. It's for my sister in Cleveland."

"It's true that you can buy peas and carrots already mixed together,
but I prefer to get them separately and do it myself."

"Bea! How did you get here before me?"

"Hah! Lookit that! Chickens that got theirs!"

"Whose carp is this? Izzim's mommy's carp?
Yessum's mommy's carp. . . ."

"Let's wrap the hamsters in velcro and throw them across the
carpet for distance."

"Outside! I want to undress!"

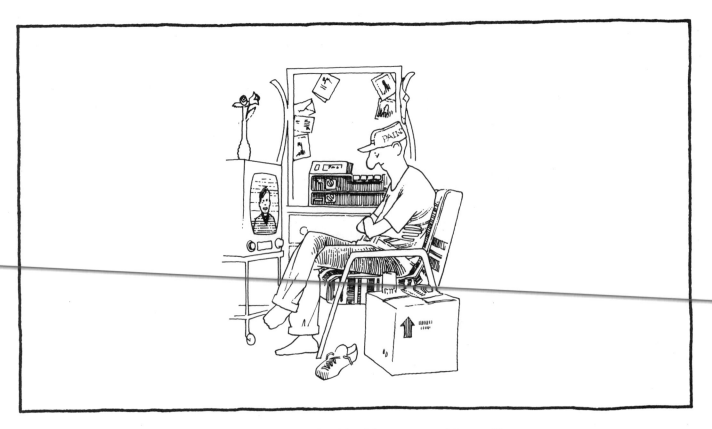

Bertram Krammer, using his videotape machine, collects
public service announcements.

*"I had a lot of single socks but I didn't become a serious collector
of them until 1967."*

Bad Dancing: Lesson One

*"This public service announcement about chasing cars was brought
to you by this station and the National Safety Council."*

"Somebody in this household has been leaking my story ideas to Fred Silverman."

"Sure, it's all my fault! Not one word about the pain, the sacrifice! I could have been a professional dancer! Did he tell you that?"

"I think we have to face the fact, Norbert, that over the years we've each grown, but in different ways."

"And here's another number I wrote about municipal bonds."

"Whatsamatta, Lady, you never got flowers by wire before?"

"Imagine being married to that during the warm months."

"Don't you realize that in the shape I'm in, exercise could be very dangerous for me?"

"Shoot! We can't eat here either."

"I'm sorry we never see him with Minnie anymore. They seemed so right for each other."

"Put the olives, lemon wedges, and pineapple slices in a bag and just act natural."

She felt a void inside.
Something was missing.
She lacked a...
She lacked a vertical hold.

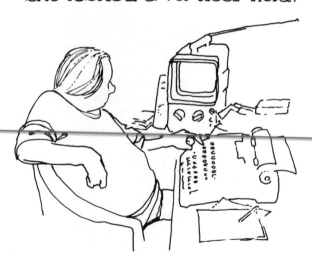

*Bea Fletcher under arrest. With the omelet you don't get a
visit to the salad bar.*

*"I can still lift my missus. It's just that I can't smile
while I'm doing it."*

"If you enjoyed dinner, Brett and I thought you might be interested in purchasing a T-shirt."

"Let's have lunch at the vending machine on the fifth floor. They vend a ham and cheese sandwich on rye up there, which is wrapped in clear plastic and has a little sticker on it that says 'fresh.' But here's the thing: On top of the sandwich they put a slice of pickle which makes for a very attractive package."

"It's you who's held me back! I might have been with the muppets only you were too cheap to pay for lessons."

Fashion Tip: Remember to accessorize your bowling wardrobe.

"Hold it, you two! You didn't think you were going to get out of
here without taking some leftovers, did you?"

M., Virgo, plain, non-drinker, hates music, dancing, sports, and people, seeks like minded F. with little or no sense of humor.